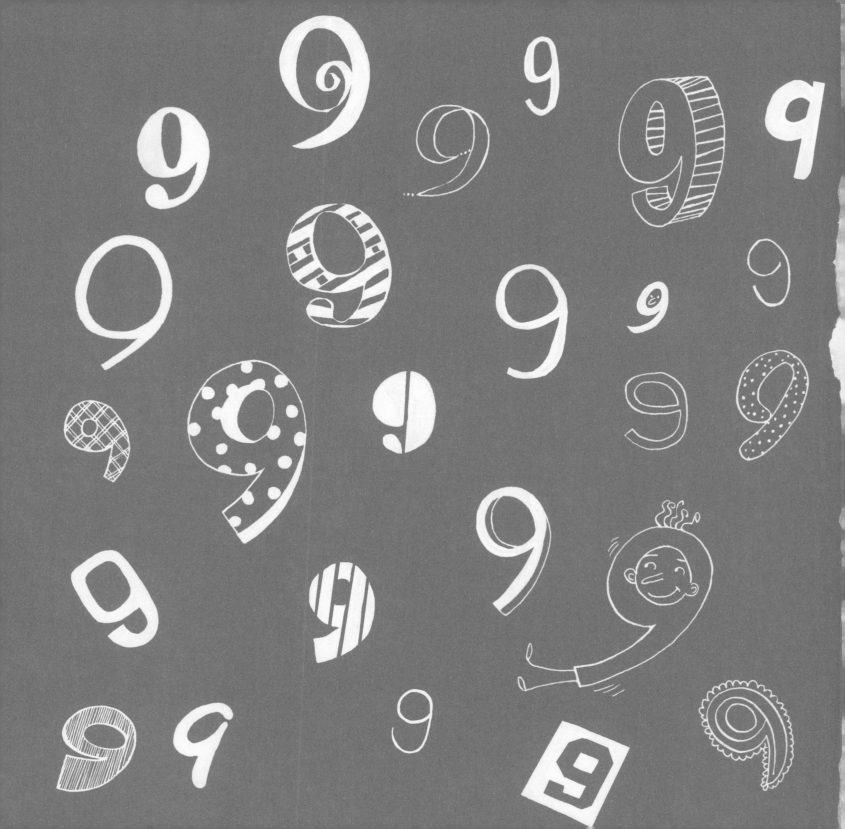

NINE 9

A Book of Nonet Poems

Irene Latham

Illustrated by

Amy Huntington

Charlesbridge

For 9-year-olds and 99-year-olds
everywhere, and for my little brother
MicaJon with so much love—I. L.

To my mom, Shirley, with much love
and admiration—A. H.

Published by Charlesbridge
85 Main Street
Watertown, MA 02472
(617) 926-0329
www.charlesbridge.com

Library of Congress Cataloging-in-Publication Data
Names: Latham, Irene, author. | Huntington, Amy, illustrator.
Title: Nine: a book of nonets / Irene Latham; illustrated by Amy Huntington.
Description: Watertown, MA : Charlesbridge, 2020.
Identifiers: LCCN 2018058513 (print) | LCCN 2019000670 (ebook) |
    ISBN 9781632898814 (ebook) | ISBN 9781632898821 (ebook pdf) |
    ISBN 9781623541163 (reinforced for library use)
Subjects: LCSH: Nine (The number)—Juvenile poetry. | Children's poetry,
    American.
Classification: LCC PS3612.A8685 (ebook) | LCC PS3612.A8685 A6 2020
    (print) | DDC 811/.6—dc23
LC record available at https://lccn.loc.gov/2018058513

Printed in China
(hc) 10 9 8 7 6 5 4 3 2 1

Illustrations done with watercolor, gouache, and colored pencil on hot press
    Arches paper with digital tweaks
Display type set in Summerica by Creative Market
Text type set in Catalina Clemente by Kimmy Design
Color separations by Colourscan Print Co Pte Ltd, Singapore
Manufactured by 1010 Printing International Limited in Huizhou, Guangdong, China
Production supervision by Brian G. Walker
Designed by Diane M. Earley

no·net \no'·net\ n a nine-line poem
in which the first line contains nine
syllables; the next line, eight syllables;
and so on until the last line has one
syllable, or the reverse, with one syllable
in the first line and nine in the last.

Nonet

Grand
poem
with nine lines—
one-syllable
first line builds toward
nine-syllable ninth line
(or the reverse). A staircase
for poets and readers alike!
(Any subject, rhyming optional.)

Engine Number 9

Hop
aboard
this train for
numerical
wheel-and-whistle songs.
Nine-a, nine-a, nine-a . . .
Butterfly net of numbers.
Nine's what remains when you subtract
one from ten or add five plus four. Nine!

Before You Were Born

For
nine months
you grew big
as a melon
inside a garden
of heartbeat and fluid.
Cells reaching, building pathways—
each day making you strong enough
to meet the brilliant, luminous world.

Counting Under the Big Top

Nine upside down is a clown called six,
who makes kids laugh at the circus.
While all the other numbers
lumber around the ring,
nine upside down blasts
from a cannon,
soars through air,
circles,
roars.

The Poem on Page 9

No
poem
dazzle-shines
like this one! See
its supermoon face?
How it commands the stage,
illuminating deep dark?
This poem transforms hearts and sky
with its star-bright glimmer-shimmer grin.

Nine Lives

Runt
is last
to suckle.
Gets lost in storm,
trapped under car hood.
Soon hisses, bites, scratches—
escapes rowdy pack of dogs.
Trembles as small hands reach, cuddle.
Eventually circles, sleeps. *Purrrrrrrrr.*

Purrrrrrrr...

Play Ball!

Glove
ready.
Pitcher winds,
ball flies across
dirt, grass, diamond sky.
Nine players like dancers
on a stage lit by starshine.
Rounding the bases, sliding home.
Home run! (And that's how the game is won.)

Nine-Banded Armadillo

This creature wears nine belts but no pants.
No socks ride its leathery legs,
yet it sports an armored coat.
It dances by moonlight
and feasts on termites,
claws *click-clicking*,
snout snuffling
in worm
dirt.

Dreaming with Pluto

Dwarf
planet.
It circles
farthest from sun,
dreaming of the day
it will regain its rank:
ninth planet. Maybe someday
Pluto's view won't be so cluttered.
We stargaze, dreaming dreams of our own.

Nine O'Clock

Let's
close our
spelling books.
Move on to math.
Our pencils scribble
numbers around circles
as Mrs. Fattig teaches
how to tell time the old-school way,
with two *tick-tock* hands and a clockface.

Nonagon

Nine
sides—all
those angles!
Kind of like an
octagon, but more.
Almost a decagon,
but not. Can you picture it?
Just imagine it's a bird's nest,
and you'll be fine when you take the test.

The Little Rock Nine

Arkansas, 1957.
Nine African American students arrive at a white school. *Integration now!* One more brick toward equality.
So many bricks to go.

Ninth President

It's
easy
to forget
William Henry
Harrison. He died
after thirty-one days
as chief. If only he'd worn
a coat and shortened his speech on
that drizzly inauguration day.

Portrait Gallery

William H. Harrison

Apollo 9

Spider and *Gumdrop* floated in space— docking, undocking. Astronauts tested equipment for days. Meanwhile the moon waited, watched as three men took essential steps toward that cosmic leap.

Game Night

Ever heard of these nine-letter words?
Paparazzi, whizzbang, schnozzle,
flapjacks, bushwhack, bamboozle.
Let's nine-i-fy our game
vocabulary
before next week's
family
Scrabble
match.

Cloud Nine

That place where happiness and grace meet.
Like a bubble, you rise and rise.
Once you get there, you don't want
to leave. But clouds are made
to shift, drift, shuffle.
Watch for rainbows
and silver
linings.
Shine!

Dressed to the Nines

Tonight we're dressed like Cinderella
and Prince Charming before the ball.
My new shoes and your bow tie
make us sparkly as stars.
But underneath we're
the same people:
smart, goofy,
hopeful,
kind.

Beethoven's Ninth

The composer's final symphony—
glorious choral masterpiece!
Clockwork of sweet strings and brass.
Rings joy, strikes wide wonder,
awakens with notes
its creator
heard only
in his
heart.

The Whole Nine Yards

Now
we've reached
the end. Nine
is the greatest
one-digit number.
Final step before ten.
Let's celebrate! Chinese "nine"
means "everlasting"—just like my
love for you. Thanks, nine, for everything.

The Whole Nine Yards About the Poems

After the introductory poem to define "nonet," there are eighteen more poems in this book. 18 ÷ 2 = 9. Also, the sum of the digits of any multiple of 9 is 9. (Example: 9 x 5 = 45; 4 + 5 = 9. And another: 9 x 15 = 135; 1 + 3 + 5 = 9. Cool, huh?) Finally, if you measure a page of this book, you'll find that it's 9 inches by 9 inches!

Engine Number 9: "Engine, Engine Number 9" is a 1965 pop song by Roger Miller. It's also a rhyme used to determine who is "it" in a game.

Before You Were Born: A human baby takes 9 months (or forty weeks) to grow inside its mother.

Counting Under the Big Top: A 9 turned upside down looks like a 6. Don't get confused!

The Poem on Page 9: Material that calls attention to something in a book (like this poem, which refers to being on page 9) is called "metafictive," or "meta" for short.

Nine Lives: Cats are said to have 9 lives because they take risks and survive. The cat in this poem was the smallest in the litter, was chased by dogs, and hid under a car in a storm—surviving it all. How many lives does this cat have left?

Play Ball!: Baseball is often called America's pastime. Teams have 9 players on the field at a time, and there are 9 innings in each game.

Nine-Banded Armadillo: There are many types of armadillos; this one is found in North America, Central America, and South America.

Dreaming with Pluto: Pluto, a dwarf planet, was considered the 9th planet in our solar system from its discovery in 1930 until 2006, when the definition of what makes a planet was changed. While it orbits the sun and is round (two of the three criteria to be a planet), it still has objects from the nearby Kuiper Belt in its orbit, so it hasn't "cleared its neighborhood," the last criterion it must meet.

Nine O'Clock: Clocks with hands that move around a face are called analog, while clocks that display the exact time in numerals are digital.

Nonagon: A nonagon is a shape with 9 sides and 9 angles.

The Little Rock Nine: The Supreme Court case *Brown v. Board of Education* found in 1954 that segregated (separated by race) education was wrong. In 1957, 9 black students enrolled in the formerly all-white Little Rock Central High School in Little Rock, Arkansas. They were treated terribly. Today, students of different races go to school together, but there is a lot more work to be done before racial equality in the United States becomes a reality.

Ninth President: William Henry Harrison won the 1840 presidential election and was inaugurated on March 4, 1841. He became sick on March 26 and died on April 4. He was the first president to die in office and served the shortest term—thirty-one days.

Apollo 9: This NASA space mission blasted off on March 3, 1969, and lasted ten days. The spacecraft included *Spider*, a lunar module, and *Gumdrop*, a command module. Astronauts James A. McDivitt, David R. Scott, and Russell L. Schweickart didn't land, but they helped pave the way for the Apollo 11 mission only four months later, when astronauts landed on the moon and walked on its surface.

Game Night: Making a 9-letter word in the game Scrabble is very difficult because each player has only seven letters at a time. But it's possible to add letters to a word already on the board—and get loads of points, too!

Cloud Nine: Being on cloud 9 means to be euphoric or excited.

Dressed to the Nines: This idiom (a phrase or saying with a meaning different from the literal words) means "dressed to perfection" or "dressed up to the highest degree."

Beethoven's Ninth: Symphony no. 9 in D Minor was the last symphony of Ludwig van Beethoven, composed between 1822 and 1824. He began to lose his hearing in his twenties and was completely deaf when he created what has become one of the most performed symphonies in the world.

The Whole Nine Yards: This idiom means "everything" or "the whole lot." In Chinese culture, the number 9 is considered lucky because the word for "nine" shares the pronunciation "jiu" with the word for "everlasting."

A last note: The word *nonet* doesn't refer only to poetry. It can also refer to a group of 9 people or things, an instrumental group with 9 players, a piece of music that has 9 parts, or a group of 9 computer data bits. Too bad there aren't 9 definitions!